I Want to Know · THE BIBLE
About

Rick Osborne and K. Christie Bowler

ZondervanPublishingHouse
Grand Rapids, Michigan

A Division of HarperCollins *Publishers*

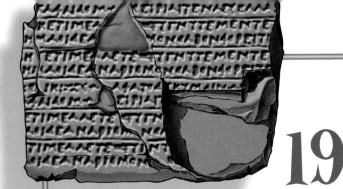

19

For Lightwave
  Managing Editor: Elaine Osborne
  Art Director: Terry Van Roon

The Bible copyright © 1998 by The Zondervan Corporation.

Artwork and Text copyright © 1998 by Lightwave
  Publishing Inc. All rights reserved.
  http://www.lightwavepublishing.com

Scripture portions taken from the *Holy Bible, New
  International Reader's Version* Copyright © 1994,
  1996 by International Bible Society.

Photos on pages 6 and 19 courtesy of Zondervan
  Publishing House.

Library of Congress Cataloging-in-Publication Data

Osborne, Rick, 1961–   .
        The Bible / Rick Osborne.
            p.   cm.—(I want to know™)
        Summary: Introduces the Bible, covering its major
    stories, favorite passages, how it was made, translat-
    ed, and preserved, and how to read, study, and apply
    its teachings.
        ISBN 0–310–22089–0 (hardcover)
        1. Bible—Juvenile literature.   [1. Bible.]
    I. Title. II. Series: Osborne, Rick, 1961–   .
    I want to know™.
        BS539.083   1998
        220.6′1—dc21   97-38952
                                                CIP
                                                AC

This edition is printed on acid-free paper and meets the
  American National Standards Institute Z39.48 standard.

Published by Zondervan Publishing House, Grand Rapids,
  Michigan 49530, U.S.A. http://www.zondervan.com

Printed in Mexico.

All rights reserved.

Building Christian faith in families

A Lightwave Production
P.O. Box 160 Maple Ridge
B.C., Canada V2X 7G1

98 99 00 /DR/ 5 4 3 2 1

Contents

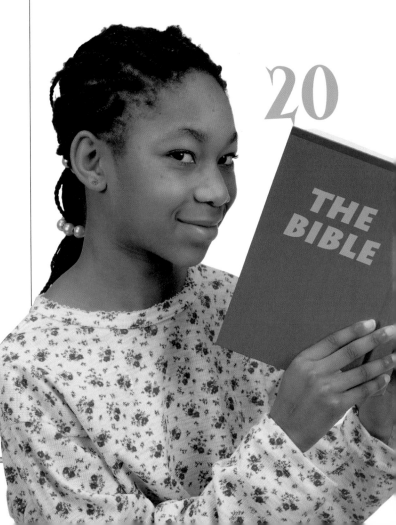

20

11

17

28

What Is the Bible?

Did you know God has a book out? His book is the most well-known, unique book ever written. It's the Bible! Why did God put this best-seller together? Here are four reasons:

His Autobiography: The Bible tells us about God's character and values, who he is and what he does, so we can begin to understand him.

His Plan: God wanted to tell us his plan for the world. You see, Adam and Eve disobeyed him and wrecked their relationship with God—and everyone else's relationship with God as well. But God had a plan to repair the relationship. The Bible tells us the story of God's plan and how he dealt with people.

A Love Letter: The Bible tells us *how* we can have a relationship with God. We all sin. You've probably noticed that. No one is perfect. God tells us how he dealt with sin and made a way for us to be together.

An Instruction Manual: God made the world to work in a certain way—a way that lines up with what he's like. It works by particular principles and rules—kind of like a computer works by certain commands and programs. The way to have the best life is to follow those rules and principles. God wrote them down for us in the Bible so we'd know how to have a great life.

Notice that all the reasons he made the Bible are for US! The Bible is all about God and us. God gave us his book for *our sakes*: for *your* sake, so you can have a wonderful life and a great relationship with him.

It makes you want to know more, doesn't it? Keep reading!

Life's Instruction Manual

Everyone wants to be happy and have a fantastic life, but how? Well, if you want to know how to operate a VCR or put together a model car, you pull out the instruction manual. So if you want to know how to have a great life, pull out the instruction manual—the Bible!

God made the world and everything in it so he knows how it works best. God gives us guidelines and principles to follow, and rules that tell us how to act and live for the best possible results.

For example, the Bible tells us not to lie because lying leads to trouble. When we lie, people eventually find out and stop trusting us. That wrecks our relationship with them. Lying spoils friendships and opportunities. To have a happy life, with good, trusting relationships and great opportunities, people need to trust us. We need to follow the rule not to lie. It's for our own good. The Bible also tells us how to handle our money, honor and be close to God, treat others, have good friendships, and much more.

Want a good life? Pull out the instruction manual. Follow it and you will have a good life. Guaranteed!

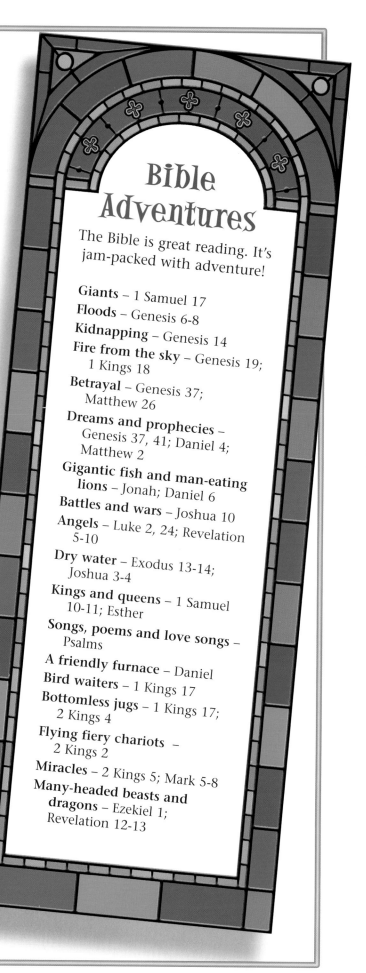

Bible Adventures

The Bible is great reading. It's jam-packed with adventure!

Giants – 1 Samuel 17

Floods – Genesis 6-8

Kidnapping – Genesis 14

Fire from the sky – Genesis 19; 1 Kings 18

Betrayal – Genesis 37; Matthew 26

Dreams and prophecies – Genesis 37, 41; Daniel 4; Matthew 2

Gigantic fish and man-eating lions – Jonah; Daniel 6

Battles and wars – Joshua 10

Angels – Luke 2, 24; Revelation 5-10

Dry water – Exodus 13-14; Joshua 3-4

Kings and queens – 1 Samuel 10-11; Esther

Songs, poems and love songs – Psalms

A friendly furnace – Daniel

Bird waiters – 1 Kings 17

Bottomless jugs – 1 Kings 17; 2 Kings 4

Flying fiery chariots – 2 Kings 2

Miracles – 2 Kings 5; Mark 5-8

Many-headed beasts and dragons – Ezekiel 1; Revelation 12-13

It's a Publishing Miracle!

Moses: *Prince, shepherd, leader—recognized as the writer of most of the Pentateuch, the first five books of the Bible.*

David: *Shepherd, musician, king—wrote many of the Psalms.*

Paul: *Religious leader—wrote about thirteen of the letters in the New Testament.*

Luke: *Medical doctor—wrote the books of Luke and Acts.*

John: *Fisherman—wrote the four books called John and Revelation.*

God is the Bible's author, but if you're picturing him typing away at a galaxy-sized computer, stop! That's not how he did it! He *inspired* the Bible. That means he worked with and through people, by his Holy Spirit, so that they wrote what he wanted. No other book has ever been written like this!

God chose people. Using their own personalities, ways of speaking, cultures and experiences, he got them to write down what he wanted to tell us. Every word they wrote is from God. "God has breathed life into all of Scripture" (2 Timothy 3:16). "No prophecy in Scripture ever came from a prophet's own understanding. It never came simply because people wanted it to. Instead, the Holy Spirit guided the prophets as they spoke" (2 Peter 1:20-21).

God chose more than forty people to write the 66 books in the Bible. Some were rich; some were poor. There were kings, poets, prophets, prisoners, musicians, philosophers, generals, farmers, teachers, priests, politicians, shepherds, a tax collector, a doctor, and a couple of fishermen. The writers also spoke different languages (Hebrew, Aramaic, and Greek) and lived in different continents (Africa, Asia, and Europe) and different times. It took over 1500 years to write the whole Bible!

Imagine getting forty people from different cultures, backgrounds, jobs, and times in history to agree on something as complicated as life, religion, and what's right and wrong! Yet the Bible's writers agree on all the main issues and more! In fact, what they wrote all fits together perfectly into the one big story of God's plan for us. Only God could have done that!

Copy Right!

The Bible was written long before paper was invented. The earliest "paper" was clay tablets. Later, dried animal skins called *parchment,* or sheets of *papyrus* made from grass-like papyrus plants were glued then rolled up into scrolls. Even later, parchment or papyrus pieces were sewn together like pages in a book.

The last book of the Bible was written 1350 years before the printing press

The Bible was copied by hand.

was invented. For all that time, books were copied by hand! This took such a long time that often a church or *synagogue* (a Jewish church) had only one copy of the Bible (or parts of it) to share.

The Jews knew the Bible was God's words and instructions. They treated the Old Testament with great respect. To keep the words correct they copied it *very* carefully. The *scribes* or copiers had rules about the kind of parchment and ink to use, how to space things, and how to ensure accuracy. They'd count the letters and words in their copies and compare them to what the rules said they should have. A copy with even one mistake was destroyed!

The New Testament copiers were non-Jews who didn't have as many rules to guide them. For hundreds of years, the job was done by monks in monasteries hunched over high desks in small, dimly lit rooms, called *scriptoriums.*

We can compare copies from different times and places and they're all the same!

בְּרֵאשִׁית֖ בָּרָ֣א אֱלֹהִ֑ים
אֵ֥ת הַשָּׁמַ֖יִם וְאֵ֥ת הָאָֽרֶץ

The Old Testament was written right to left in Hebrew, with a few sections in Aramaic.

Οὕτως γὰρ ἠγάπησεν ὁ
θεὸς τὸν κόσμον, ὥστε

The New Testament was written in Greek like this, with a sprinkling of Aramaic words.

The Bible Is Amazing!

The Bible is one-of-a-kind! It was written in a way no ordinary book could possibly be written and still make sense. Here's why it's amazing:

It's Number One: The Bible has been read by more people, in more languages, than any other book. It was the first book to be printed on a printing press and one of the first to be translated into another language. Millions of Bibles are sold or given out every year around the world in 2000 languages and dialects.

It's the Best Kept: We have over 5000 old hand-written copies or parts of copies of the New Testament. We also have tens of thousands of pieces of copies of the Old Testament! They show that the Bible we have today is the same as when it was written!

Old pens or quills were made from feathers.

It Tells It Like It Was: Many people have said the Bible couldn't be God's words because it's full of people and places they thought were made up. But, as archaeologists examine more old places, what the Bible says is shown to be completely right!

It Tells It Like It Will Be: The Bible has a lot of prophecy in it. Prophecy is God telling us what's going to happen. Many prophecies in the Bible came true over a thou-

Ancient copies of the New Testament were words on papyrus like this.

2. When copies from many different places and times say the same things, it shows they're accurate.

Until 1947, our oldest piece of the Old Testament was from 800 years after Jesus. Then a shepherd boy in Israel found clay jars hidden in a cave. They contained what we call the *Dead Sea Scrolls.* Among them was a scroll of Isaiah from 200 years before Jesus! People compared this manuscript with what we already had—it's almost exactly the same!

We have over 5000 ancient copies or pieces of copies of the New Testament. We also have a whole New Testament from only 300 years after the last book was written!

sand years later! Only God knows the future.

The Bible is so completely one-of-a-kind that no other book is even in the contest!

The Bible Is Accurate

How do we know that the copies of the Bible are accurate? We compare.

1. The older the *manuscript* is, the more accurate it is—it's been copied fewer times so there are fewer chances of mistakes.

Monks copied the Scriptures by hand for hundreds of years.

From "ΑΓΑΠΗ" to "LOVE"

"Ουτωζ γαρ ηγαπησεν ο Θεοζ τον κοσμον." Or "Houtos (who-toes) gar agapasen (ay-gap-ay-sen) ho theos (thay-oss) ton (tone) kosmon (kosmoan)." **Say what?** Those are Jesus' words. You didn't recognize them? Well, they're in Greek. The story of how they got from that to "For God so loved the world" is fascinating!

The Old Testament was translated from Hebrew into Greek 200 years before Jesus by 70 scholars. It's called the *Septuagint* (meaning "seventy") or LXX (the Roman numeral for seventy). Since the New Testament was written in Greek too, most people could understand the whole Bible. But over the next several hundred years, Latin became the common language, and people couldn't read it as easily. So a man named Jerome made a translation into Latin. His translation, the *Vulgate,* was finished in A.D. 405.

Meanwhile, others were translating the Bible into their own languages such as Coptic, Syriac, Ethiopic, Gothic, and Armenian. Some languages had never been written before so translators even had to make up alphabets. In the late 1100s the Bible started to be translated into European languages, like Spanish and French.

For hundreds of years the authorities only allowed the clergy—priests and pastors—to have Bibles. In 1374 John Wycliffe said everyone should be able to read the Bible for themselves. His followers made the first English translation, the *Wycliffe Bible,* around 1395. The authorities were upset and made it illegal to own an English Bible without permission! But that didn't stop people—even though the translators were often jailed or killed.

Around 1456 the Bible was the first book printed on a printing press. Copies became cheaper to own, and Bibles were quickly printed in many different languages. Translations took off! In 1611 King James the First had the best Bible scholars put together the most famous English Bible, the *King James Version.*

There are several major English translations today: New International Version, New King James Version, New Revised Standard Version, and the New Living Bible.

By the end of 1995, at least part of the Bible had been translated into more than 2100 languages, the whole Bible had been translated into 276 languages, and more translations are still being made. The Bible is a worldwide book!

The first printed Bible was made on a printing press similar to this one.

The First Book Printed

A very famous man was born around A.D. 1400 (actually he wasn't famous yet) in Mainz, Germany. Johann Gutenberg was trained as a goldsmith, but he was tired of goldsmithing and was experimenting with printing. Printing at that time was done by cutting words and pictures into large wood blocks. The blocks were inked, and parchment, or the newly discovered paper, was pressed onto the ink.

Gutenberg had a better idea. He thought, "What if I cut each letter onto a separate piece of wood or metal? I could use the same pieces, or type, over and over. I could rearrange them into new words, sentences and pages. *Moveable type* would let me print better and cheaper books!" It was a revolutionary idea!

By 1456 he had printed the first ever books—around 180 *Gutenberg Bibles* in Latin—using moveable type.

His Bible was a great success and soon everyone was printing this same way!

What's in It?

The Gospels according to Matthew, Mark, Thomas . . . Hold it! There's no Gospel of Thomas, is there? Actually there is, but it's not in the Bible. It's not part of the *canon*—the books that are accepted as Scripture.

The Bible is made up of sixty-six books. Why only these? Well, God helped people recognize the books that were his.

The Old Testament

No one is sure how the canon of the Old Testament was decided. The *Pentateuch* or *The Law*—the first five books of the Bible—was recognized as belonging in the Bible more than 500 years before Jesus. *The Prophets* and *Psalms* were seen as

canonical 100 to 200 years before Jesus. Jesus talked about "the Law, the Prophets, and Psalms" as inspired by God and part of the Bible. Ninety years after Jesus' birth, a Jewish council declared the Old Testament canon to be what we have today.

Some copies of Bibles have other books in them called *The Apocrypha*. These books have good things in them, but they're not recognized as inspired by God or part of the canon.

The New Testament

After the Apostles died, all kinds of new writings claimed to be true. But some taught false things. The people needed to know what to

Can you find the books of the Bible in this library?

believe, so the church leaders had to discover which books and letters were from God. One of the keys in deciding was whether the book was known to have been written by an apostle or someone who worked closely with them, like Luke. As early as A.D. 170 the four Gospels (Matthew, Mark, Luke, and John) were recognized as canonical. Next were Paul's letters, then Revelation, Acts, and the letters of other apostles. In A.D. 367 an important pastor, Athanasius, wrote a letter listing the canon of the New Testament.

Just over 300 years after Jesus' death and resurrection, all the books of the Bible were the same as we have today. The canon was set and closed!

The Bible Library

Now what order should the books be in? Alphabetical? Longest to shortest or vice versa? Nope. How about topical? Sure, they did it like two libraries: Old Testament and New Testament. They put history first, then the other types of writing, then prophecy.

Here's the Old Testament Library—all the history books from Genesis to Esther. Then the poetic books, Job to the Song of Songs. Next comes the major prophets with lots to say—Isaiah to Daniel—then the minor prophets with less to say—Hosea to Malachi. And that's how Christians organize the Old Testament.

The New Testament Library is similar. First come the history books, the Gospels and Acts. Then come the letters that were written during or after Acts. Paul's letters are first, then come Hebrews and the other letters. Finally, there's prophecy, the book of Revelation.

Old Testament Books | **New Testament Books**

Historical
Genesis
Exodus
Leviticus
Numbers
Deuteronomy
Joshua
Judges
Ruth
1&2 Samuel
1&2 Kings
1&2 Chronicles

Poetic
Job
Psalms
Proverbs
Ecclesiastes
Song of Songs

Major Prophets
Isaiah
Jeremiah
Lamentations
Ezekiel
Daniel

Minor Prophets
Hosea
Joel
Amos
Obadiah
Jonah
Micah
Nahum
Habakkuk
Zephaniah
Haggai
Zechariah
Malachi

Historical
Matthew
Mark
Luke
John
Acts

Paul's Letters
Romans
1&2 Corin-
thians
Galatians
Ephesians
Philippians
Colossians
1&2 Thessa-
lonians
1&2 Timothy
Titus
Philemon

Other Letters
Hebrews
James
1&2 Peter
1,2&3 John
Jude

Prophecy
Revelation

The Greatest Story

The Bible tells one big story about God creating everything so he could have a wonderful Father/child relationship with us. But everything was wrecked, so God put his plan into action to make it all better. Here's the story in a nutshell.

It began when only God existed—God the Father, Son, and Holy Spirit. God made everything! He made people, Adam and Eve, to be like his children. He wanted to be our Father and have a fantastic relationship with us. He gave Adam and Eve a beautiful Garden to live in with all good things, and one rule: Don't eat fruit from this one tree! But Satan, an important angel who became God's enemy, disguised himself and lied to them. They ate the fruit! That was sin, so God sent them out of the Garden. Sin separates us from God. As a result, everyone born since then has been born sinful and separated from God too. Satan and sin spoiled God's plan to be a father to us. But don't worry. The story is just beginning!

Adam and Eve had children who had children . . . . Soon the world was full of sinful people. God was very sad. He said, "I'll destroy everyone." But God found one man who loved him, Noah. God told Noah to build a huge boat or *ark*. He sent two of every animal into the ark with Noah's family. It began to rain. We're talking **RAIN!** Forty days and nights later, only those in the ark were alive.

Noah's children had children who. . . . God chose Noah's descendant Abraham with his wife Sarah. He told them he'd be their God and sent them to a land he promised to give their children forever. Off they went to Canaan. But Abraham and Sarah couldn't have children. Then God gave them a son, Isaac, and promised that one of his descendants (the *Messiah*) would bless the whole world!

Isaac's son Jacob, or *Israel*, had twelve sons and one daughter. Jacob gave his favorite son, Joseph, a special coat. Joseph's brothers were jealous. They sold him as a slave into Egypt.

Adam and Eve sin

God gives Abraham and Sarah a son

Joseph's family come to Egypt

Joseph kept loving and obeying God. Years later God helped him explain a dream to the *Pharaoh* or king of Egypt—a huge famine was coming! Pharaoh told Joseph to get Egypt ready. When Joseph's family came for food, Joseph invited them to live in Egypt.

The *Israelites*, all Israel's descendants, came and had children who had children who . . . . They increased until the new Pharaoh got worried. He made them slaves and ordered their baby boys killed. That's when Pharaoh's daughter rescued an Israelite baby, Moses. Moses grew up in the palace, then he ran away to the desert. Years later he saw a bush burning without burning up. God spoke to him from it, "Go to Egypt. Tell Pharaoh to let my people go!" God sent ten plagues to show he was stronger than Egypt's false gods. In the last plague the eldest child in every family was to die. But the Israelites killed lambs and put the blood on their doorways so God would pass over their houses. The lambs died instead of the eldest children. This was called the *Passover*. That night Pharaoh let God's people go!

The Israelites left in a huge *Exodus*. God led them into the desert and gave Moses the *Ten Commandments* and the Law telling them how to please God and have a good life. Then God led them to the land he'd promised Abraham long ago. Under the leader Joshua, the Israelites defeated the wicked people living there and settled in. When the Israelites followed God's Law, things went well. When they didn't, their enemies conquered them. They'd cry to God for help, and God would send a judge or leader to defeat their enemies. One judge, Deborah, told Barak to gather an army to fight Commander Sisera. The army defeated the enemy! Another judge was Samson. God gave him amazing strength. Alone, he killed 1000 men who came to capture him!

Years later the Israelites asked God for a king. Their first king, Saul, fought their enemies, the Philistines. A giant Philistine, Goliath, mocked God. Young David fought him with a sling and stones. He won! He loved God with all his heart. His son Solomon was wise, but later

The Israelites leave Egypt   *The Israelites conquer Canaan*   *David fights Goliath*

God saves Daniel from the lions

Jesus is born in a stable

Jesus heals the sick

A horrible death

Saul meets Jesus

Jesus is coming back

kings didn't love God like David did. God sent *prophets* to remind his people to follow his Law. They didn't listen. So God let enemies take them prisoner far away to Babylon.

Daniel was an Israelite or *Jew* who loved God and became a leader in Babylon. He prayed to God even when it was against Babylon's law. So he was thrown into a lions' den. But God kept Daniel safe! Later, the ruler let some Jews return to their land. Now God's people decided to obey God's Law. Everything was ready for the key part of God's plan!

God sent an angel to Mary and her fiancé, Joseph, saying Mary would have God's baby. Mary had a little boy, *Jesus*, just as God had said. Jesus was God, but he became a person like us because he loved us. He was part of God's plan—the promised Messiah. God told simple Jewish shepherds and non-Jewish wise men about his Son's birth, showing he'd come for *everyone*.

Jesus grew up in Nazareth. When he was about thirty, he began the job God had given him. At the Jordan River he was baptized. Then God led him into the desert. Satan tempted Jesus to do things his way instead of God's, just like he had done to Adam and Eve. But Jesus quoted from the Bible and refused.

Jesus taught about God and his kingdom. He showed that God loved people by healing the sick and feeding the hungry. He taught how to have a good relationship with God. Jesus chose twelve men to be his special followers or *disciples*. The religious leaders were afraid the crowds would follow Jesus instead of them because he taught new ideas like,"God loved the world so much that he gave his one and only Son. Anyone who believes in him won't die but will have eternal life" (John 3:16). The leaders thought the key was to obey the Law, not believe in Jesus. They decided to get rid of Jesus but were afraid of a riot.

Judas, one of Jesus' disciples, offered to help the leaders arrest Jesus. Around the time of the Passover celebration (remember the Passover?) Judas led guards to arrest Jesus. Jesus was tried for saying he was God's Son. The punishment was death. Jesus was beaten and led out to be crucified, a horrible death. Jesus asked his Father to forgive the people because they didn't know what they were doing. Then he said, "It's finished." He'd done everything God sent him to do!

After he died, friends put his body in a tomb. The Jews guarded the tomb so no one could steal Jesus' body and say he'd risen from the dead. But on the third day the tomb was empty! Jesus appeared to many people, proving he was alive again.

God had accepted his death (instead of ours) as payment for our sins! That meant the separation begun by Adam and Eve was ended. All people could be God's children!

Jesus sent the Holy Spirit to help his followers tell the world about him. The Jewish leaders tried to stop them, but nothing worked. One leader, Saul, searched out Jesus' followers to have them killed. One day Jesus appeared to Saul and asked why he was persecuting God's people. From that day Saul changed his name to Paul. Paul traveled around the world telling people about Jesus. He started churches and wrote letters to help new believers live as God wanted. He also explained the teachings of the Bible and Jesus.

John, another disciple, was sent to an island prison for following Jesus. Jesus gave him a message for the Church. It's in *Revelation* in our Bible. Jesus promised to come back and take us to be with him in a new heaven and earth. There'll be love and happiness there. No more sadness or pain! We'll be with God as his children just as he planned before the world began. What a party that will be!

The Bible tells the best story ever written. And every part is true!

Archaeology Digs It

Imagine this: 300 years from now no one believes there is a place called California and no one has heard of Walt Disney! Let's say just one book talks about California. Because there's so little evidence people don't believe the writer. Then someone starts digging and finds Magic Mountain! They find other books about California and pictures of Walt Disney. Now they believe the writer and they take her seriously.

That's what happened with the Bible. For a long time, it was the only book that talked about certain places and people, so scholars didn't believe that those people or places ever existed. Then along came *archaeologists* who study anything old to learn about the past. In the last eighty years, they have found other writings mentioning the same things as the Bible. They have also dug up ancient ruins that confirm what the Bible says.

Wherever people live they leave things behind—clay pots, weapons, writing, and buildings. Some of these things are kept safe in the ground for *thousands* of years. By studying these ancient things, archaeologists learn about their owners.

They might study a hill. Long before it was a hill, people built a town there. Over time, dirt, garbage, and new building projects added layers. Maybe the town was destroyed by enemies. Another town was built on the ruins. Archaeologists dig down through the hill's layers, often finding several towns built on top of each other. Archaeologists compare what they find with things from other places. They discover when the things were made, who lived there and for how long, who they did business with, and so on.

Thousands of sites have been excavated all over Bible lands. And guess what! **Nothing** has been found to prove the Bible wrong! Nada! Zilch! Zero!

Archaeologists use tools like these to uncover ancient towns.

Digs like this teach us about the past.

Digging Up the Truth

Check out what people used to think and what archaeologists have found!

⌕ **Thought:** Moses couldn't have written the first Bible books (Deuteronomy 31:24) because in his time, no one knew how to write yet.

Found: A "Black Stele" (a carved black rock) three hundred years older than Moses' time with laws written on it. Also, tablets from the excavated city of Ebla written a thousand years before Moses.

⌕ **Thought:** There was no Sodom, Gomorrah, and other cities Genesis says were in the Jordan valley. No one lived there in Abraham's time.

Found: The Ebla tablets mention the same cities in the same order as Genesis 14. And ruins of more than seventy towns and cities from Abraham's time and older have been found there.

Scholars translate ancient writing on clay tablets like this.

⌕ **Thought:** The Hittites (Genesis 23:10; Joshua 11:1-9) didn't exist.

Found: A Hittite city and tablets from Egypt that mention the Hittites.

⌕ **Thought:** Joshua didn't really conquer Canaan (Joshua 10-11). He and the Israelites moved in peacefully.

Found: Tablets from Canaan kings asking Egypt for help against Habiru (Hebrew) invaders.

⌕ **Thought:** Pontius Pilate wasn't a real person. If he was, he shouldn't have been called "Prefect."

Found: A large stone saying, "Pontius Pilate, Prefect of Judea."

⌕ **Thought:** King David was a legend. He didn't really exist.

Found: An inscription from David's time that refers to the "House of David" and the "King of Israel."

There are many other examples of things being found that agree with what the Bible says.

Parts adapted with permission from Josh McDowell's books A Ready Defense *and* More Evidence That Demands a Verdict.

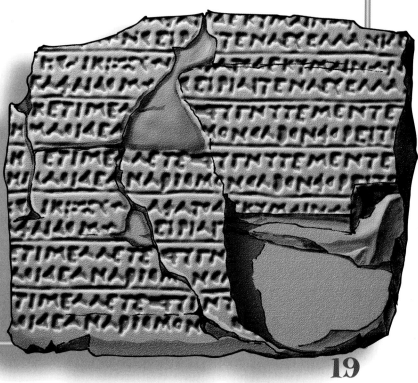

God's Treasure Map

A copper scroll was found with the *Dead Sea Scrolls*. It described *treasures* hidden around the countryside! The experts studied it to make sure it was for real and to figure out exactly where the treasures should be.

Landmarks have changed over the 2000 years since the scroll was written, so the experts also studied other scrolls and histories to help them compare how things *were* to how they *are* now. They probably copied and memorized the scroll's clues and directions so they'd have the information even when they were away from the scroll.

The Bible is just like the copper treasure scroll. It was written by someone who knows what he's talking about—God! He made life and knows how it works. He knows how to help us find the life-treasures he's prepared for us—things like good families, friendships, happiness, freedom, safety, success, and comfort. He gave us a "scroll" with everything we need to find his treasures for a great life. Just as we'd study an ancient scroll or map, we can study God's map.

"God has breathed life into all of Scripture. It's useful for teaching us what is true . . . for correcting our mistakes . . . making our lives whole again. . . training us to do what is right. By using Scripture, God's people can be completely prepared to do every good thing" (2 Timothy 3:16–17). Here's how to learn from God's "treasure map."

Read

The experts had to read the scroll to understand what it was about. Reading the whole Bible helps us understand what God and his book are all about. It gives us the overall story of God's plan and why Jesus came. It also shows us who God is and what he's like.

Study

The experts' second step was to study the scroll. They spent time with it, looked at it in sections, and did whatever else would help them understand it. They'd study one particular treasure, find out all about it, and make sure they understood the instructions.

We can use the Bible the same way. We can pick a topic we need to know more about. We can study that topic by looking up the places in the Bible that talk about it. By studying the Bible we can understand *why* God says things like, "Be honest. Use words to encourage, not destroy." We'll discover all kinds of things!

Memorize

The experts probably memorized key parts of the scroll. That way they could refer to them when they were out hunting for the treasure. We memorize Bible verses for the same reason. We need to know how to find the treasure in any situation and do the right thing. For example, say you get upset and say unkind things. That's definitely not a treasure! Want the treasure of a great friendship? Memorize Ephesians 4:29: "Say only what will help to build others up and meet their needs. Then what you say will help those who listen." Now the next time you're tempted to be unkind with your words you'll know what to do. And hey! Your friendship becomes even better—a treasure!

You see, the Bible is not a book just for knowledge. No way! It's a book for living. It's real. God's treasure map is there for us to use and learn from. So read, study, memorize—and keep digging up treasures!

No matter what your age or your style, there's a Bible out there to make you smile.

Read the Treasure Map

When you learn to sing you begin with "do, re, mi." What about when you start reading the Bible? Well, starting at the beginning is a very good place to start! But remember, the Bible is like a library. Don't try to take on the whole library in one go! Tackle one book at a time.

There are lots of ways to read the Bible.

You might start by reading the Old Testament history books Genesis and Exodus. Then read the New Testament history books Luke and Acts. Then go to one of the letters. A good one is James. These books will give you an overview of God's plan.

Treasure Trove

First Find Plan

Introduction to the Bible

This plan is your first look at the Bible's treasures. It's good for those who haven't really read the Bible before.

Beginnings
Genesis

Forming a Nation
Exodus

Jesus' Story
Luke

The Church Begins
Acts

Practical Living
James

Digging Deeper

For serious treasure hunters. This plan hits the treasure payload and is a good expansion of the First Find Plan.

Numbers 8-27
Deuteronomy 6, 7, 34
Joshua 1-10, 24
Judges 1-7, 13-16
Ruth
1 Samuel 1-21, 23-31
2 Samuel 5-7
Psalms 23, 32, 100, 103, 130, 139
1 Kings 3-5, 8-12
Proverbs 1-3, 10, 15
1 Kings 16-18
2 Kings 2-5, 7, 12, 18-20, 22-24
Isaiah 53 (It's about Jesus' job)
Jeremiah 52:1-16
Daniel 1-6
2 Chronicles 36:22-23
Ezra 1, 3, 6
Nehemiah 1-8
Esther

John
Acts (If it's been a while, you might want to read Acts again.)
Romans 1-8, 12-14
1 Corinthians 12-15
2 Corinthians 4-5, 9
Galatians 5-6
Ephesians 4-6
Philippians 2-4
1 Thessalonians 4-5
1 Timothy 6
2 Timothy 2, 4
Titus 3
Hebrews 11
1 Peter 1-3
2 Peter 3
1 John
Revelation 1-3, 20-22

We read the Bible to help us grow in a relationship with God. Since the Bible is God's book, spending time reading the Bible is spending time with God. By reading it daily, we're getting in touch with him and getting to know him.

You see, the Bible is no ordinary book! Oh no! The Holy Spirit, who helped God's chosen writers say what God wanted, is still working through the Bible. He can make it come alive to us. No, it won't get up and walk around or do flips. But it just might "talk." The Holy Spirit helps us understand what the words and stories mean. The Bible "comes alive" because the Holy Spirit uses it to say something we need to hear, answer a question we have, or help us understand just what we're going through. God "breathes" into our lives through his words in the Bible. This makes the Bible totally unique: God uses the words written thousands of years ago to help us in our lives *today*. That's one of the Holy Spirit's jobs! (Remember 2 Timothy 3:16–17?)

We've given you some Bible reading plans. Also, if you want to jump around in the Bible a bit and read some favorite parts, check out pages 24–25. They tell you where to find the famous stuff in the Bible. Choose your plan, and happy treasure hunting!

Treasure Teasers

Bible hot spots.

Sssmoking!
Jeremiah 36

The Sword
Ephesians 6:10-18

Kings Please Leaf
Judges 9:1-15

Clouds in Church
Exodus 40:1-2, 17-38

No Sleeping in Church
Acts 20:7-12

House Cleaning
Mark 11:15-19

Longest, Loudest Church
Revelation 4-5

Plagues
Exodus 7:8-12:30

Spies
Numbers 13

Noses and Toeses
1 Corinthians 12

The Best of the Bible

Think of your favorite book or story. You probably know it pretty well. And you probably have favorite parts too, parts you love hearing over and over and over again. Well, the Bible's been around a *l-o-o-o-n-g* time! In that time people have had many favorite parts. Some of them become favorites for just about everyone. Here are some of the all-time favorites!

Famous Old Testament Verses

The Shepherd's Psalm
Psalm 23
Thanks Psalm
Psalm 100
God Knows You
Psalm 139
Seek Wisdom
Proverbs 2:3-4
Trust God
Proverbs 3:5-6
Wise Request
1 Kings 3:1-15
Time for Everything
Ecclesiastes 3:1-8
Jesus Will Suffer
Isaiah 52:13-53:12
Let's Talk
Isaiah 1:18
The Christmas Verse
Isaiah 9:6
Good Plans for You
Jeremiah 29:11-14

Famous New Testament Verses

The Blesseds
Matthew 5:1-12
Don't Worry
Matthew 6:25-34
Great Commands
Mark 12:28-34
Nicodemus's Lesson
John 3:16
Rest for the Weary
Matthew 11:28-30
Spirit Fruit
Galatians 5:22-26
Love's the Thing
1 Corinthians 13
Body Parts
1 Corinthians 12:12-31
Spiritual Armor
Ephesians 6:10-18
God Dries Tears
Revelation 21:1-5

The Lord's Prayer

Our Father in heaven, may your name be honored.
May your kingdom come.
May what you want to happen be done on earth as it is in heaven.
Give us today our daily bread.
Forgive us our sins, just as we also have forgiven those who sin against us.
Keep us from falling into sin when we're tempted.
Save us from the evil one.

(Matthew 6:9-13)

The Ten Co

1. Don't put any other gods in place of me.

2. Don't make any statues of gods. . . . Don't bow down and worship them.

3. Don't misuse the name of the Lord your God.

4. Remember to keep the Sabbath day holy.

5. Honor your father and mother.

Famous Bible Stories

Remember what we said about God's reasons for giving us the Bible? The Bible is full of exciting, fascinating stories to read and enjoy. But they're there for another reason, too. They teach us how life works, what happens when we obey God or when we don't, the power of prayer, how God cares for us . . . and on and on it goes! So here are some great stories. Enjoy them and find the treasure in them that God has for you.

God Creates – *Genesis 1*
Adam & Eve – *Genesis 2-3*
The Flood – *Genesis 6-9*
Everyone Babbles – *Genesis 10-11*
Son Sacrifice – *Genesis 22:1-19*
Dream Ladder – *Genesis 28*
Golden Calf – *Exodus 32:1-35*
Red Sea Drought – *Exodus 14*
Jericho Falls – *Joshua 6:1-27*
Timid Gideon – *Judges 6:1-7:24*
Jawbone Judge – *Judges 13:1-16:31*

Young Samuel – *1 Samuel 1:1-28; 3:1-21*
David and Goliath – *1 Samuel 17*
Bird Waiters – *1 Kings 17*
Prophetic Showdown – *1 Kings 18*
Fiery Chariot – *2 Kings 2*
Your God's Mine – *Ruth 1-4*
Futile Fiery Furnace – *Daniel 3:1-30*
Non-man-eating Lions – *Daniel 6*
Fish Food – *Jonah*
Save a Nation – *Esther*
Amazing Birth – *Luke 2:1-40; Matthew 2*
Young Jesus – *Luke 2:41-52*
Feed the Famished – *Mark 6:32-44*
Walk on the Wet Side – *Matthew 14:22-33*
Fish Pays Taxes – *Matthew 17:24-27*
Alive Again – *John 11:1-46*
Good Samaritan – *Luke 10:30-37*
Lost Son – *Luke 15:11-32*
Zacchaeus – *Luke 19:1-10*
Holy Spirit Fire – *Acts 2:1-24*
Saul Sees the Light – *Acts 8:1-3; 9:1-19*
Animals in Sheets – *Acts 10:1-35*
Jail Break – *Acts 16:16-40*

mandments

6. **Don't commit murder.**

7. **Don't commit adultery.**

8. **Don't steal.**

9. **Don't give false witness against your neighbor.**

10. **Don't long for or envy anything that belongs to your neighbor.**

Study the Treasure Map

Okay! You're reading the Bible and discovering what this "treasure scroll" is all about. Ready for serious digging? Want to discover specific treasures, like how to pray? Or have great friendships?

Think of our copper roll expert. He or she studies, cross-checks, then acts: off for the treasure! Ready to try it? Let's do a *topical study*.

1 Get a notebook and call it your *Treasure Chest*. You'll fill it with the gold and jewels you find in the Bible!

2 Choose a "treasure" to study, say *love*.

3 Pray. God understands his book better than anyone. So it's important to ask for his help.

4 Find a part of the Bible that teaches about your topic. A great section on love is 1 Corinthians 13. Read it. Think about it. Ask questions. For example, what does "is not self-seeking" mean? Write down your thoughts.

Everything in the Bible fits together, and the Bible has oodles to say about love. Let's check it out by using some *tools of the trade*.

5 Many Bibles have *cross-references*, little notes beside verses that point to other verses on the same topic. In our picture, look up the cross-references for 1 Corinthians 13:5. You can follow the topic's trail from verse to verse like following a trail in the woods. Try 1 Corinthians 10:24 too. What does "is not self-seeking" mean?

Cross Reference

1 CORINTHIANS 13:1

Love

And now I will show you the most excellent way.
13 If I speak in the tongues of men and of angels, but have not love, I am only a resounding gong or a clanging symbol. ²If I have the gift of prophecy and can fathom all mysteries and all knowledge, and if I have faith that can move mountains, but have not love, I am nothing. ³If I give all I posess to the poor and surrender my body to the flames, but not have love, I gain nothing.

13:1 "ver 8; S Mk 16:17
13:2 "ver 8; S Eph 4:11; S Ac 11:27
"1Co 14:2
"S 2Co 8:7
"1Co 12:9
"Mt 17:20; 21:21
13:3 "Lk 19:8; S Ac 2:45
"Da 3:28
13:4 "1Th 5:14
"1Co 5:2
13:5
"S 1Co 10:24
"S Mt 5:22 "Job 14:16,17; Pr 10:12;17:9; 1Pe 4:8
13:6 "2Th 2:12
"2Jn 4; 3Jn 3,4
13:7 "ver 8, 13

⁴Love is patient, love is kind. It does not envy, it does not boast, it is not proud." ⁵It is not rude, it is not self-seeking, it is not easily angered, it keeps no record of wrongs. ⁶Love does not delight in evil but rejoices with the truth. ⁷It always protects, always trusts, always hopes, always perseveres.

⁸Love never fails. But where there are prophecies, they will cease; where there are tongues, they will be stilled; where there is knowledge, it will pass away. ⁹For we know in part and we prophesy in part, ¹⁰but when

6 A *concordance*. Most Bibles have a small one in the back. Concordances list Bible words, and verses that use them. From our pic-

Concordance

LOVE (BELOVED LOVED LOVELY LOVER LOVER'S LOVERS LOVES LOVING LOVING-KINDNESS)

Ge 20:13 'This is how you can show your *l*
22: 2 your only son, Isaac, whom you *l*,
29:18 Jacob was in *l* with Rachel and said
29:20 days to him because of his *l* for her
29:32 Surely my husband will *l* me now."
Ex 15:13 "In your unfailing *l* you will lead
20: 6 showing *l* to a thousand generations
20: 6 of those who *l* me
21: 5 'I *l* my master and my wife
34: 6 abounding in *l* and faithfulness.
34: 7 maintaining *l* to thousands.
Lev 19:18 but *l* your neighbor as yourself.
19:34 *L* him as yourself,
Nu 14:18 abounding in *l* and forgiving sin
14:19 In accordance with your great *l*,
Dt. 5:10 showing *l* to a thousand generations
5:10 to those that *l* me
6: 5 *L* the LORD your God
7: 9 generations of those who *l* him
7: 9 keeping his covenant of *l*

Mt 3:17 "This is my Son, whom I *l*;
5:43 '*L* your neighbor and hate your
5:44 *L* your enemies and pray
5:46 you *l* those who *l* you, what reward
6: 5 for they *l* to pray standing
6:24 he will hate the one and *l* the other
12:18 the one I *l*, in whom I delight;
17: 5 "This is my Son, whom I *l*;
19:19 and '*l* your neighbor as yourself.' "
22:37 '*L* the Lord your God
Ro 5: 5 because God has poured out his *l*
5: 8 God demonstrates his own *l* for us
8:28 for the good of those who *l* him.
8:35 us from the *l* of Christ?
8:39 us from the *l* of God that is
12: 9 *L* must be sincere.
12:10 to one another in brotherly *l*.
16: 8 Greet Ampiatus, whom I *l*
1 Co 2: 9 prepared for those who *l* him" –
4:17 my son whom I *l*, who is faithful
4:21 or in *l* and with a gentle spirit?
8: 1 Knowledge puffs up, but *l* builds up
13: 1 have not *l*, I am only a resounding
13: 2 but have not *l*, I am nothing
13: 2 but have not *l*, I gain nothing

ture, look up a couple of verses. Read the verses around them to see how they fit into what the writer is saying. Who is loving? How is love shown? Write your answers in your *Treasure Chest*.

7 *Bible dictionaries* are tools too. Like concordances, they're alphabetical and easy to use. Just look up "love" and there you are, love stuff. (Check out our picture.) If you're into computers you'll strike gold! Many study tools are on disc or CD ROM. Do a *search* or *find* on "love" and just see what the

computer kicks onto your screen!

Dig deep. Treasures are there for the taking!

8 *Act!* Now you get to live out what you've learned. God is ready to help.

Bible Dictionary

Love

LOVE

Love is the grandest theme of Scripture. It is a divine motivation. It moved God to reach out to the lost; and it enables the lost to look up in response, as well as to reach out to others. What the Bible says about love cannot help but enrich our lives.

OT　1. **The Hebrew words**
　　2. **God's love for man**
　　3. **Man's love for God**
NT　4. **The Greek words**
　　5. **God's love in Christ**
　　6. **Man's love for God**

8. Summary. God is portrayed in Scripture as the one who, moved by love, initiates a relationship with human beings. God's love prompts his free decision to reach out to sinful humanity.

In the OT, God's love is focused on the covenant people of Israel, and his love is demonstrated by his acts for them. In return, God's OT people are called to show their love for God by commitment to him alone and by obedience to his commands.

In the NT, the full scope and meaning of God's love is unveiled.

Being a good friend
1 Samuel 18:1; 20:1-42;
1 Corinthians 15:33;
Proverbs 17:17

Honesty
John 8:32; 14:6; Psalm 15:1-3; Proverbs 3:3;
Exodus 20:16

Money
Matthew 6:19-34;
Proverbs 3:9-10;
1 Timothy 6:10

Love
1 Corinthians 13; 1 John 4:7-21; John 15:12-13;
Matthew 22:39

Prayer
Matthew 6:5-15; Mark 11:23-26; Luke 18:9-14

Learn It by Heart

Combination locks. Telephone numbers. Birth dates. What do these have in common? They're all things we memorize—with good reason. We do it so we can get into our lockers, call home and friends, and remember the special days of people we love.

The Bible is the same. We memorize parts of it for very good reasons. When we're out living, things come up that we need help with. We can't always get to life's instruction manual to look them up. But if we have verses in our heads and hearts we can find them quickly and *eureka!* We know what to do. We can apply the Bible's instructions right there and then.

Sunday schools often have contests and prizes for the most verses memorized. But don't forget the *reason* we memorize. It's not just to get points or win contests. Nope. It's much more important than that!

The world can be a dark place, with confusion, questions, sin, temptation, and disappointments. There are lots of choices to make, lots of paths to take. Which one is right? Which leads to God's treasure? If the paths are all dark it's hard to see which is safe or which has rocks and holes. Enter the Bible! God calls it a light. "Your word is like a lamp that shows me the way. It is like a light that guides me" (Psalm 119:105). The Bible can show us the right choice to make, the path that leads to a treasure. Memorizing key verses keeps that light right where we need it, in our hearts and heads. It helps us know the best way to live.

So let's memorize and light our lamp!

Memory Tips

The key isn't just to memorize the words. It's the *meaning* you want. Here are some steps once you've chosen your verse:

1. Pray for God's help. Look up your verse in the Bible and read it.
2. Think about what the verse means.
3. Read it again. Think of where you could use it. At home? With friends? Doing schoolwork? On the playing field? With your piggy bank?
4. Read the verse again. You want to get the verse inside you, into your heart and your thinking. You want it to be part of you so that when a situation comes up you can pull it out of your brain's filing cabinet right away.
5. Read the verse a few more times out loud so you can hear it.
6. Close your Bible and say it out loud without looking.
7. Do this until you feel it's in your heart and you know where you can use it.

There you are! You have a jewel locked away in your mind/heart treasure chest. Now you simply review the verse every once in a while and ask God to remind you of it when you need it.

You're on the path to a treasure-filled life!

Memory Jewels

Friendship – Proverbs 17:17 "Friends love at all times. They are there to help when trouble comes."

Temptation – 1 Corinthians 10:13 "You are tempted in the same way all other human beings are. God is faithful. He will not let you be tempted any more than you can take. But when you are tempted, God will give you a way out so that you can stand up under it."

Kids and Parents – Ephesians 6:1–3 "Children, obey your parents as believers in the Lord. Obey them because it's the right thing to do. Scripture says, 'Honor your father and mother.' That is the first commandment that has a promise. 'Then things will go well with you. You will live a long time on the earth.'"

How You Talk – Ephesians 4:29 "Don't let any evil talk come out of your mouths. Say only what will help to build others up and meet their needs. Then what you say will help those who listen."

When You Need Wisdom – James 1:5 "If any of you need wisdom, ask God for it. He will give it to you. God gives freely to everyone. He doesn't find fault."

When You Mess Up – 1 John 1:9 "But God is faithful and fair. If we admit that we have sinned, he will forgive us our sins. He will forgive every wrong thing we have done. He will make us pure."

The Life-Changing Book

The treasures we find in the Bible can change our lives. As we learn to live by its instructions, we become more like Jesus. And Jesus promised us a helper, the Holy Spirit, who would teach us about God and help us obey him.

Jesus died for our sins so that we could have God as our loving heavenly Father. When we pray and ask God to forgive us, he does. Then, with the help of the Holy Spirit and God's grace, we become more like he wants. That's what the Bible is all about.

Q **Does the Bible tell us what God wants us to do?**

A Yes. In the Bible, God's Word, God tells us what he wants us to do and how he wants us to live. Although there are a lot of stories and information in the Bible, God's four main instructions for our lives are: (1) believe in Jesus and trust him every day, (2) obey Jesus and do what he says, (3) love God and others, (4) be fair and honest and live for God without being proud about it.

Q **Will people write about us in a special Bible, too?**

A There is only one Bible (or "revelation from God"), and it has already been written. But remember, the Bible is far more than a collection of stories about people who lived a long time ago—it's God's message about Jesus; it tells how we should live today. The Bible also tells us about the future, not just the past. So in one sense, we are in the Bible. We are important in God's plan. Also, the Bible tells us that those who believe in Jesus have their names written in the "Lamb's Book of Life"—that's another book that God has. It tells who will live with God in heaven.

Q Why do we study the Bible?

A It's important to study the Bible because the Bible is God's message to us and studying it helps us understand it better. If you want to learn more about basketball, you study basketball. Studying the Bible helps us find out how to live and what God wants. When we only read the Bible (without studying it), we may not see the meaning right away. Studying helps us learn lessons for life. We learn God's will so we can obey him. Studying the Bible is like reading a story many, many times. Each time you see something different and learn more.

Q What is the Bible's biggest story?

A The biggest story is the story of Jesus. In fact, the whole Bible tells his story about God creating people and saving them from sin. Jesus came to the world to die in our place and pay the penalty for our sins. If we trust in Jesus as Savior, God gives us eternal life. The Old Testament Bible writers told us that Jesus would be born, live, die, and rise again. Even the sacrifices described in the book of Leviticus show us what the death of Christ would be, the perfect "Lamb of God who takes away the sin of the world." No matter where you look in the Bible, you can learn about Jesus. Have you put your faith in him?

Taken from 101 Questions Children Ask About God, *the Livingstone Corporation and Lightwave Publishing Inc., 1992 and* 102 Questions Children Ask About the Bible, *Tyndale House Publishers, 1994.*

The Best Way of All

God gave us the Bible so we could know him, learn his plan, and have great lives!

Remember, God is love. First Corinthians 13 (remember the study?) says that love is never selfish. So everything in God's book is for our good, not his. When God tells us to be honest (Proverbs 10:9), honesty makes our lives better. Loving God with all our hearts (Deuteronomy 6:5) makes us happier. Honoring our parents (Ephesians 6:1-3) means "things will go well with us." The key to a happy life is obeying God. That doesn't mean we'll never be sad. But God will always be with us, helping us to learn and make it through.

Check out Psalm 119. It's all about the good things that come from loving and obeying God's Word. "Teach me to live as you command, because that makes me very happy" (Psalm 119:35). God doesn't tell us to study his book because there's a test. He tells us to do it because it has everything we need for fulfilled, happy, contented lives—in every part of our lives from home to school, sports to money, friends to feelings. What a great deal!